Tools

Search

Notes

Discuss

MyReportLinks.com Books

Go!

CIVILIZATIONS OF THE ANCIENT WORLD

ANCIENT ROME

A MyReportLinks.com Book

GIVLIO CESARE

DEBORAH KOPS

MyReportLinks.com Books

an imprint of

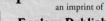

Enslow Publishers, Inc.

Box 398, 40 Industrial Road
Berkeley Heights, NJ 07922
USA

CN 937
Kops

MyReportLinks.com Books, an imprint of Enslow Publishers, Inc. MyReportLinks® is a registered trademark of Enslow Publishers, Inc.

Library of Congress Cataloging-in-Publication Data

Kops, Deborah.
  Ancient Rome / Deborah Kops.
    p. cm. — (Civilizations of the ancient world)
"A MyReportLinks.com Book."
Includes bibliographical references and index.
ISBN 0-7660-5255-9
1. Rome—Civilization—Juvenile literature. I. Title. II. Series.
DG77.K67 2005
937—dc22
                                                  2004017527

Printed in the United States of America

10 9 8 7 6 5 4 3 2 1

To Our Readers:
Through the purchase of this book, you and your library gain access to the Report Links that specifically back up this book.
The Publisher will provide access to the Report Links that back up this book and will keep these Report Links up to date on **www.myreportlinks.com** for five years from the book's first publication date.
We have done our best to make sure all Internet addresses in this book were active and appropriate when we went to press. However, the author and the Publisher have no control over, and assume no liability for, the material available on those Internet sites or on other Web sites they may link to.
The usage of the MyReportLinks.com Books Web site is subject to the terms and conditions stated on the Usage Policy Statement on **www.myreportlinks.com**.
A password may be required to access the Report Links that back up this book. The password is found on the bottom of page 4 of this book.
Any comments or suggestions can be sent by e-mail to comments@myreportlinks.com or to the address on the back cover.

Photo Credits: © Ancient World Mapping Center, p. 19; © Corel Corporation, pp. 1, 3, 10, 13, 16, 18, 22, 27, 30, 32, 38, 44; © Detroit Institute of Arts, p. 12; © The Louvre Museum, pp. 21, 28; Clipart.com, p. 37; Leptismagna.com, p. 43; MyReportLinks.com Books, p. 4; Pietro da Cortona, c. 1643, p. 15; University of Erlangen, p. 34; University of Oregon, p. 41.

Cover Photos: Coliseum, Ruins, Hemera.com; Statue of Augustus, © Corel Corporation.

Contents

ANCIENT ROME

MyReportLinks.com Books
Great Books, Great Links, Great for Research!

The Internet sites listed on the next four pages can save you hours of research time. These Internet sites—we call them "Report Links"—are constantly changing, but we keep them up to date on our Web site.

Give it a try! Type http://www.myreportlinks.com into your browser, click on the series title, then the book title, and scroll down to the Report Links listed for this book.

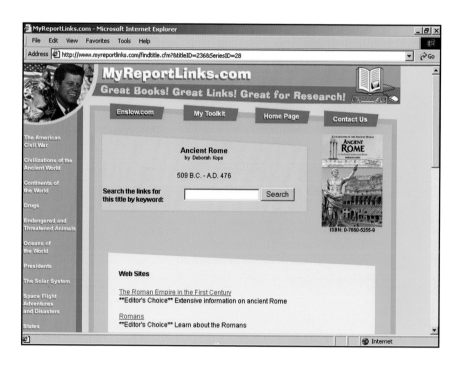

The Report Links will bring you to great source documents, photographs, and illustrations. MyReportLinks.com Books save you time, feature Report Links that are kept up to date, and make report writing easier than ever!

Please see "To Our Readers" on the copyright page for important information about this book, the MyReportLinks.com Web site, and the Report Links that back up this book.

Please enter **VRO1916** if asked for a password.

The Internet sites described below can be accessed at http://www.myreportlinks.com

*EDITOR'S CHOICE

▶ The Roman Empire in the First Century

This Web site from PBS provides a look back into ancient Roman life and culture. Learn about Rome's emperors, its social order, marriage and divorce laws, and more.

*EDITOR'S CHOICE

▶ Romans

This Web site from the British Broadcasting Company contains information and articles on ancient Rome.

*EDITOR'S CHOICE

▶ Colosseum: A Gladiator's Story

On this interactive Web site from the Discovery Channel, you can learn about the Colosseum in Rome. Take a tour of the Colosseum and view animated gladiator battles.

*EDITOR'S CHOICE

▶ Secrets of Lost Empires: Roman Bath

This PBS site provides an in-depth look at the complex and sophisticated system of tunnels, arcades, arches, and aqueducts built by the ancient Romans to secure clean drinking and bathing water.

*EDITOR'S CHOICE

▶ Internet Ancient History Sourcebook: Rome

The Internet Ancient History Sourcebook is a site that offers a comprehensive history of ancient Rome as well as many links to other sites about this ancient civilization and culture.

*EDITOR'S CHOICE

▶ Louvre Museum

The Louvre Museum in Paris is one of the world's great art museums. At the museum's Web site, click on "Collections" and then "Greek, Etruscan, and Roman Antiquities" for a look at some ancient Roman works of art.

The Internet sites described below can be accessed at
http://www.myreportlinks.com

▶**Ancient Art: Rome**

On this Web site from the Detroit Institute of Arts, you can view several ancient Roman artifacts. On view are sculptures as well as everyday items used by the people of ancient Rome.

▶**Ancient Rome**

Take an online tour of Roman art and architecture on this academic Web site. Beginning with the Etruscans and moving through the imperial age, there is information covering a wide range of subject matter as well as photographs.

▶**Cleopatra: A Multimedia Guide to the Ancient World**

Learn about ancient Rome and its significance from this Art Institute of Chicago Web site. Information on Rome's emperors, art, architecture, and culture is included as well as a time line and maps.

▶**Daily Roman Life**

The ancient Romans were first governed by what is called the Twelve Tables and subsequently by the Gracchi laws. Learn more about the Romans and their culture and government from this University of Vermont site.

▶**Europe Image Library**

This site is a collection of full-color photographs depicting life in ancient Rome. Images of homes, theaters, baths, aqueducts, art, and landscapes are included.

▶***The Gallic Wars***

This site provides a full-text version of *The Gallic Wars* by Julius Caesar. He wrote this account while on an extended military campaign in Gaul. Read firsthand what this important Roman general and leader did and thought.

▶**Gladiators**

You will find information about gladiators on this PBS site, including a description of early gladiatorial combat through its heyday and ending with the slave uprisings that contributed to the decline of the games in A.D. 404.

▶**History for Kids: Ancient Rome**

The Roman Empire was one of history's largest and most powerful empires. At this Web site designed for kids, you can find out about the history, religion, government, and people of ancient Rome.

Report Links

The Internet sites described below can be accessed at http://www.myreportlinks.com

▶**The Later Roman Empire**

Diocletian was Roman emperor from A.D. 284 to 305. He split the empire into two parts to make it easier to govern, and he also appointed a co-emperor. This site covers how he restructured the economy and military and introduced social and religious reforms.

▶**Leptis Magna**

This site offers information on the history and culture of Leptis Magna, an ancient city in what is today Libya that was founded by the Phoenicians and later became part of the Roman Empire.

▶**On the Roman Emperors**

This site is a collection of biographies of Roman emperors and members of their families. Family trees, information on significant battles, maps, and a catalog of Roman coins are also included.

▶**Perry-Castañeda Library Map Collection: Historical Maps of Europe**

This Web site contains numerous historical maps of Europe, including maps related to the Roman Empire.

▶**Pompey**

Pompey was a great statesman and general of the late Roman Republic. He worked with Caesar and Crassus to expand Rome's territory and make it safe from pirates. This site contains Plutarch's biography of the general.

▶**Roman Art and Architecture**

This site contains a wide variety of photographs depicting ancient Roman people, life, and emperors. You will find images of architecture, art, wall paintings, temples, funerary monuments, and reliefs from both the Republican and Imperial periods.

▶**Roman Monuments**

A collection of photographs taken of ancient sites in the city of Rome can be found on this Web site. The images are accompanied by explanatory text.

▶**The Roman Principate: 27 B.C.–A.D. 312**

This university Web site covers the time period of Roman history between 27 B.C. and A.D. 312. Learn about Augustus, Marcus Aurelius, gladiators, and more.

Report Links

The Internet sites described below can be accessed at http://www.myreportlinks.com

▶ **The Romans**

This BBC site provides an excellent overview of the ancient Romans and their influential history, which extended into Britain. Included is information on families, leisure activities, the military, engineering, and religion.

▶ **Rome: Republic to Empire**

This academic Web site includes information on ancient Roman clothing, houses, leisure, social classes, government, emperors, armies, and more.

▶ **Rome at Its Height**

Learn about the Roman Empire from this site, which offers information on its geography, government, military, culture, and religion. A link is provided to "The Deeds of the Divine Augustus," the emperor's own account of his accomplishments.

▶ **Savage Fashion: Animals and Attitude in Ancient Rome**

The Circus Maximus and the Colosseum were sites of well-planned animal shows that Roman emperors staged for the public. Learn more about the animals and where they came from on this Smithsonian site.

▶ **Secrets of the Dead: The Great Fire of Rome**

Who or what caused the Great Fire of A.D. 64 that nearly leveled Rome? This PBS site attempts to answer those questions by uncovering ancient secrets and examining clues.

▶ **Social Position and Food in the Roman Empire**

Differences in economic class and geographical location affected the quality and quantity of food available to ancient Romans. This site examines what the ancient Romans ate and includes information on utensils, feasts, and military food.

▶ **Voyage Back in Time: Ancient Greece and Rome**

This site about ancient Greece and Rome has lots of helpful information on what life was like in these civilizations. Learn about agriculture, government, music, entertainment, family life, and much more.

▶ **Warrior Profile: Romans**

Learn about Rome's military structure and its soldiers. This site explains the transition that soldiers experienced going from local protectors in the Republic to world aggressors during the Roman Empire.

Any comments? Contact us: **comments@myreportlinks.com**

Time Line

509 B.C.	—The Romans defeat the Etruscan king Tarquin the Proud and establish the Republic.
c. 440 B.C.	—The Twelve Tables, the Republic's laws, are published.
264–241 B.C.	—First Punic War: Rome defeats Carthage, in north Africa, and adds islands of Sicily, Sardinia, and Corsica.
218–202 B.C.	—Second Punic War: Carthaginian general Hannibal marches from Spain to Rome but is defeated by the Roman commander Publius Scipio Africanus at the Battle of Zama.
146 B.C.	—Romans destroy Carthage, which later becomes a Roman colony; Greece becomes a Roman province.
48 B.C.	—Julius Caesar defeats Pompey and two years later begins his rule of Rome.
44 B.C.	—Caesar is murdered, and civil war erupts.
31 B.C.	—Octavian, Caesar's great-nephew, defeats Marc Antony and Cleopatra to become sole ruler of Rome.
27 B.C.–A.D. 14	—Octavian/Augustus becomes the first emperor of the Roman Empire. His peaceful reign ushers in the Pax Romana, or peace of Rome, in which Roman and Greek culture spread throughout the empire.
A.D. 14	—Tiberius succeeds his stepfather, Augustus, as emperor.
A.D. 30	—Jesus of Nazareth is crucified.
A.D. 43	—The emperor Claudius begins the conquest of Britain.
A.D. 70	—The emperor Titus crushes the Jewish revolt, and the Jewish Diaspora begins.
A.D. 79	—Mount Vesuvius erupts, destroying the Roman cities of Pompeii and Herculaneum.
A.D. 98–A.D 117	—Under Trajan's rule, the Roman Empire is at its greatest size.
A.D. 122	—Hadrian builds defensive wall across northern border of Britain.
c. A.D. 125	—Hadrian rebuilds the Pantheon, originally constructed in 27 B.C.
A.D. 286	—Diocletian divides the empire into eastern and western parts.
A.D. 330	—Constantine moves the capital to Constantinople.
A.D. 476	—The Goth king Odoacer removes Romulus Augustulus as ruler, bringing an end to Roman rule of the western Roman Empire.

Chapter 1

CAESAR'S DECISION

In January 49 B.C., the Roman general Julius Caesar had to make a difficult choice. His command as governor and head of the armies in Gaul (what is today France and Belgium) was officially coming to an end. The Roman Senate, the governing body made up of members of Rome's leading families, demanded that Caesar give up his armies there and return to the city of Rome. This tall, fair-skinned man was a military hero and one of the most powerful people in the Roman Empire. At the time, Rome was stronger than any other power in Europe. Greece, once the brightest political star in the ancient Mediterranean world, had become a Roman province.

◀ Julius Caesar was one of ancient Rome's greatest generals, and his leadership inspired the loyalty of the men in his command.

A few years before Caesar faced his difficult decision, Caesar's rival, Pompey, had become extremely powerful in Rome's government. A struggle between Caesar and Pompey had been growing, and now the Senate decided to show its support for Pompey by demanding that Caesar leave his army in Gaul. Caesar knew that if he did as the Senate asked and crossed the small Rubicon River between Gaul and Italy without his army, his political career would probably be over.[1] The general's other choice was to ignore the Senate's demand, bring his army into Italy, and challenge Pompey for the leadership of the empire.

Caesar and Pompey had not always been rivals. Caesar's daughter, Julia, was Pompey's wife, and ten years earlier, they had shared the rule of Rome with a third man for one year in what was known as the First Triumvirate. When their terms as leaders were over, Caesar was appointed military commander and governor of the Roman province that included northern Italy and southern Gaul. Pompey, with the support of the Senate, became sole consul, or chief magistrate, the most powerful member of government.

Crossing the Rubicon

Caesar was not content to quietly rule his province, however.[2] Instead, he took his army into central and then northern Gaul. For eight years, this dedicated and energetic general and his army fought the independent peoples of Gaul until they conquered all of Gaul for the Roman Empire. The Romans were the first people in the ancient world to have a professionally trained army, and Caesar's campaigns proved his military genius. Somehow Caesar also found the time to write a dramatic account of his victories, *Commentaries on the Gallic Wars,* which contributed to his fame and glory.

Back   Forward   Stop   Review   Home   Explore   Favorites   History

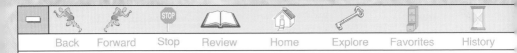

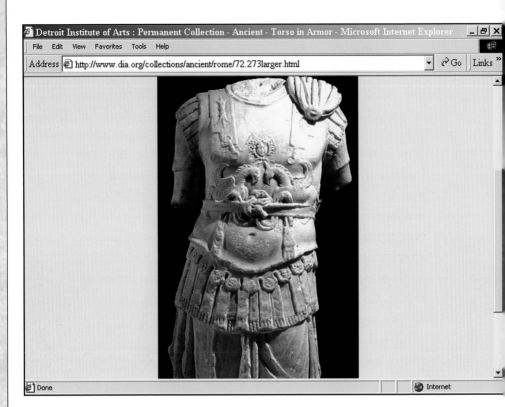

File   Edit   View   Favorites   Tools   Help

Address http://www.dia.org/collections/ancient/rome/72.273larger.html   Go   Links

Detroit Institute of Arts : Permanent Collection - Ancient - Torso in Armor - Microsoft Internet Explorer

Done   Internet

This statue of a Roman soldier's torso bears intricate carvings that show the armor worn by the Roman military in ancient times.

On January 10, 49 B.C., Caesar made the decision to enter Italy with his men. According to legend, as he crossed the Rubicon with his army, he cried out, "Let the dice fly high!"[3] He was hoping that fate would be kind to him, just as people do when they throw dice in a game. And he was willing to accept the consequences of his decision. As it turned out, the consequences were enormous: Caesar's decision, which thrust the Roman Empire into civil war, changed the course of Roman history.

FROM REPUBLIC TO EMPIRE

For a year and a half, Caesar and Pompey fought for leadership of the Roman Empire, plunging it into a civil war. In a remarkable series of military campaigns, Caesar defeated Pompey's armies in Italy and in Spain, which was part of the empire, and forced Pompey to flee to Greece.[1] There on June 6, 48 B.C., the two armies fought their final battle in Pharsalus, in northern Greece. That battle proved to be Caesar's greatest victory against Pompey, who fled the battlefield and escaped to Egypt.

Caesar's Brief Rule

When Pompey arrived in Egypt, however, he was murdered on the orders of the Egyptian pharaoh, or king. Even without Pompey, Caesar continued to draw resistance.

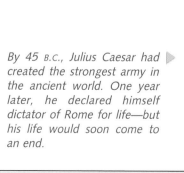

By 45 B.C., Julius Caesar had created the strongest army in the ancient world. One year later, he declared himself dictator of Rome for life—but his life would soon come to an end.

It took Julius Caesar until October 45 B.C. to destroy his remaining enemies in Macedonia, a kingdom north of Greece; Asia Minor, the peninsula between the Black Sea and Aegean Sea that is today part of Turkey; and Spain.

By then, Caesar had created the strongest and most effective army in the world.[2] But he also was smart enough to realize that he would need the support of the many people he had just conquered if his rule was to be effective. The Roman historian Velleius Paterculus (c. 19 B.C. to A.D. 32) described Caesar's great triumph as well as his generosity: "Victorious over all his enemies, Caesar returned to Rome and, a thing incredible, pardoned all who had borne arms against him."[3]

▷ Dictator for Life

The great Roman general was hungry for political power as well as military power. In 44 B.C., he appointed himself dictator for life and began appearing in public on a gold-covered chair, as if he were king. His actions angered the members of Rome's most prominent families, who were used to sharing power with the country's leader through political appointments and by serving in the Senate. Even though Caesar had brought about reforms and helped to secure the vast reaches of the empire, critics resented his power. They wanted to maintain the empire's democracy, and they were afraid that Caesar would destroy it. On March 15, 44 B.C., a group of men who had once been his friends stabbed Julius Caesar to death in a public theater where the Senate was meeting.

Caesar was fifty-five years old when he was murdered. One of the most talented men to lead ancient Rome, he was a superb military commander and a gifted writer. But he also helped to destroy Rome's republican form of government, which had lasted for five hundred years.[4]

The Early Years of the Republic

The ancient Romans created a legend to explain the birth of their country. It begins with Aeneas, the Trojan hero already a part of Greek mythology. In order to escape the destruction of the city of Troy, Aeneas flees to Italy. There he begins a family line that will eventually produce kings. Twin brothers from the family, Romulus and Remus, are left on the banks of the Tiber River, which runs through Rome. They are rescued by a wolf and helped by a shepherd. Later the brothers have an argument, and Romulus kills Remus. Romulus eventually founds the city of Rome on the banks of the Tiber, where he had been rescued.

▲ *The legend of Rome's founding is the subject of this painting, which depicts the shepherd Faustulus rescuing the twins Romulus and Remus, who were abandoned on the banks of the Tiber River.*

▲ *The Etruscans, who once ruled Rome, strongly influenced early Roman culture. This sarcophagus, a stone coffin embellished by sculpture, is an example of the Etruscans' magnificent artistry.*

People have been living in the low hills surrounding Rome since at least the tenth or eleventh century B.C. By the seventh century B.C., Rome was an established city-state, which consisted of the city and the surrounding region. It was ruled by Etruscan kings from Etruria, to the north. Under their leadership, Rome was expanding its territory and developing a warlike culture.

In 509 B.C., the Romans rebelled against the last Etruscan king, Tarquin the Proud, and founded a republic.[5] Under a government led by two elected consuls and the Senate, the Romans enlarged their empire by conquering their neighbors. By about 270 B.C., they were in control of the entire Italian peninsula and were ready to challenge the other powers on the Mediterranean Sea.

The Struggle Between Rome and Carthage

In 218 B.C., Rome clashed with Carthage, an empire on the north African coast, southeast of Italy, for the second time in about forty years. The problem began when Carthage looked to expand its territory westward into Spain. The Romans challenged the Carthaginians, and war erupted.

Rome's north African enemy sent a young and fiery general named Hannibal to invade Italy. Hannibal went on an extraordinary six-month march from Spain to Italy, crossing the steep Alps mountains with over twenty thousand men, six thousand cavalry (soldiers on horseback), and a small herd of war elephants.[6] Considered one of the greatest generals of all time, Hannibal defeated Roman armies in Italy that were much greater in number. But the Romans continued to battle Hannibal and his army for over a decade. Then in 202 B.C., a gifted young commander for Rome named Publius Scipio led an army to Africa, forcing Hannibal to leave Italy and defend Carthage. Scipio's army delivered a final crushing blow at the Battle of Zama, defeating Carthage for good. Rome was now master of the western Mediterranean world.

Rome Conquers the Eastern Mediterranean

During the next few decades, Rome sent its armies eastward. By 168 B.C., Rome had conquered Macedonia. In 146, Corinth, an important commercial center of Greece, led a revolt to protest Rome's growing power in its region. The Romans destroyed that great city and made Greece a province of Rome. Almost a century later, before Pompey

and Caesar plunged Rome into civil war, Pompey pushed the boundaries of the empire even farther east to include Judaea and the former kingdom of Syria.

▶ The Reign of Augustus

Rome's first emperor was Julius Caesar's great-nephew, whom Caesar had adopted as a son. He was later called Augustus, a Latin word that means "respected," but his given name was Octavian. Although Octavian was only eighteen when Caesar was killed, he was ambitious. By the time he was twenty-one, he began sharing the leadership of the empire with Marc Antony, who had been Caesar's main commander. By 34 B.C., Antony and Octavian were rivals. Antony had a powerful ally on his side—Cleopatra, the queen of Egypt, who was Antony's lover.

In 31, when Antony and Cleopatra moved troops to Greece, Octavian's navy, led by Agrippa, trapped them at Actium, a strip of land in coastal western Greece. Antony and

◀ In this famous statue of Augustus, the creator of the Pax Romana stands in a triumphant pose like one often used in sculptures of great athletes.

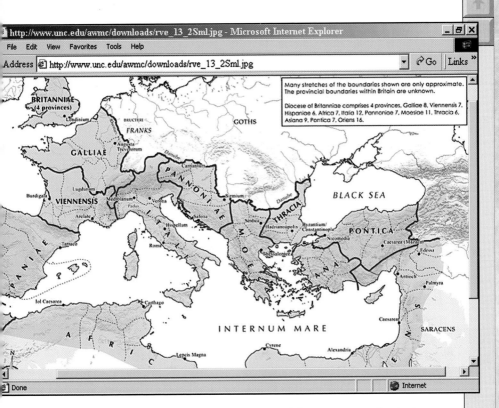

Address: http://www.unc.edu/awmc/downloads/rve_13_2Sml.jpg

Many stretches of the boundaries shown are only approximate. The provincial boundaries within Britain are unknown.

Diocese of Britanniae comprises 4 provinces, Galliae 8, Viennensis 7, Hispaniae 6, Africa 7, Italia 12, Pannoniae 7, Moesiae 11, Thracia 6, Asiana 9, Pontica 7, Oriens 16.

BRITANNIAE (4 provinces)
FRANKS
GOTHS
GALLIAE
VIENNESSIS
ITALIA
PANNONIAE
THRACIA
BLACK SEA
PONTICA
SPANIAE
INTERNUM MARE
SARACENS

▲ This map shows the lands that were part of the vast Roman Empire in A.D. 69.

Cleopatra fled to Egypt and, deciding that they were doomed, they killed themselves. Octavian was now the leader of the Roman world. Within a year, that empire included Egypt. Rome now commanded the lands of the Mediterranean and the Middle East.

The Senate honored Octavian in 29 B.C. by making him *imperator,* Latin for "commander." Two years later, the Senate gave Octavian the name *Augustus* and officially made him the head of the government. Historians view this moment as the end of the Republic and the beginning of the Roman Empire.

Pax Romana

Remembering Caesar's fate, Augustus, the Roman Empire's first emperor, treated the members of the Senate with respect, giving them the impression that he shared power with them. Although power was never returned to the people as it had been during the days of the Republic, Augustus accomplished a great deal during his reign. He granted the provinces local control and allowed different ethnic groups to practice their own customs. He improved the network of roads within the empire and taxed Rome's citizens more fairly. A period known as the Pax Romana, or Roman peace, began with the reign of Augustus and continued for nearly two hundred years. During this period, Roman culture flourished as it spread.

Trajan Stretches the Empire

The Roman Empire reached its greatest size under the emperor Trajan's rule, from A.D. 98 to 117. An experienced army commander, Trajan liked the action of the battlefield. In 106, he conquered Dacia, north of the Danube River, in what is now Romania. Farther east, Trajan won Armenia from the Parthians, leaders of the Persian Empire, in 114. From there his army conquered northern Mesopotamia (present-day Iraq) and advanced all the way to the Persian Gulf. This adventurous emperor's conquests were celebrated by Rome, where the 100-foot-high marble Trajan's Column was built to honor him.

Not every Roman citizen benefited from the enlarged empire, though. Many gave up small farms to serve in the army. When they returned from war, they moved to a city and joined a growing population of poor people. Others had trouble paying the taxes that were used to support Rome's military operations.

Tools   Search   Notes   Discuss   Go!

The emperor Hadrian strengthened the borders of the empire by stationing military garrisons on its frontiers. He is perhaps best remembered for the wall, which now bears his name, that he had built across Britain's northern border.

▷ Hadrian Strengthens the Borders

Hadrian, the emperor who ruled after Trajan, realized that the endless borders of the enormous Roman Empire had become difficult to defend. To strengthen the places where he thought Rome might be attacked by its enemies, he added permanent bases for the army. His most famous work on the frontier was Hadrian's Wall. In 122, Hadrian had this 73-mile (118-kilometer) fortified wall built across the northern border of Roman Britain to keep out the barbarian tribes beyond.

A tall and elegant man with a full beard, Hadrian was a practical ruler. He concentrated on helping the government work more smoothly and gave the Romans two decades of peace before he died in 138.

For the rest of the second century, Rome continued to prosper in the hands of the capable emperors Antoninus Pius and Marcus Aurelius. The Roman army spread Roman culture throughout the empire, encouraging even those in the far reaches of the empire to live as Romans did. In this way, the people in lands that had been conquered by Rome came to feel like Romans themselves. By 212, all free people living in the empire, which stretched from Britain in the west to Arabia in the east, were granted citizenship. But during the third century, the Roman Empire began to decline as civil wars, invasions, and economic problems threatened its prosperity and security.

▲ *Constantine became the emperor of a reunited Roman Empire in A.D. 324 and moved the empire's capital east.*

Diocletian Reorganizes the Empire

When Diocletian came to power, in 284, the empire was in need of reorganizing.[7] During the half century before his rule, there had been at least twenty emperors, and many of them had died violently. Still more violence erupted on Rome's borders. Germanic tribes in the north threatened to invade the empire. In the east, the Sassanid people of Persia took Mesopotamia, and the Dacians won their independence.

To help bring stability, Diocletian divided the Roman Empire into eastern and western regions and appointed three men to help him run it. He also doubled the number of provinces in order to make it easier to collect taxes. In 305, when Diocletian was in poor health, he officially gave up his position as emperor.

Constantine Builds a New Capital

A power struggle followed Diocletian's rule. The winner was Constantine, who became the sole ruler of a reunited empire in 324. He was a very forceful leader who broke with tradition in two important ways. First, he embraced and encouraged the spread of Christianity throughout the empire, even though he continued to tolerate other beliefs. Second, in 330 he moved the empire's capital from Rome east to Byzantium, an ancient city later renamed Constantinople in his honor. (It is now Istanbul, Turkey.)

Constantine's peaceful reign saw the building of Christian churches throughout the empire, from Rome to Jerusalem. He also rebuilt the capital, which was near important trade routes and was easy to defend against Rome's Persian enemies to the east.

The End of the Roman Empire

After Constantine's death in 337, Germanic tribes from the north continued to threaten the empire. To make matters worse, the relationship between the eastern and western regions of the empire began to break down. This was more serious for the west because the east was much wealthier and contributed more to support the empire. In 395, when the emperor Theodosius died, the empire split in two. Each region had its own emperor.

In 439, one Germanic tribe, the Vandals, captured the city of Carthage on the coast of north Africa and established the first independent kingdom inside of the empire. By 475, the Goths, another Germanic tribe, had created a kingdom in Gaul and Spain. The next year, German troops who had lived among the Romans and fought in their army suddenly revolted and elected a man named Odoacer as their leader. He made Italy his kingdom, bringing the western half of the Roman Empire to an end. The year 476 has come to signify the fall of the Roman Empire.

Although the Roman government had been toppled, the churches helped to preserve Roman culture and offer some protection to the Roman people. The eastern half, which became known as the Byzantine Empire, lasted until 1453. It survived by bargaining with its enemies and integrating them into the empire instead of fighting them.[8]

THE REPUBLICAN GOVERNMENT AND ITS PEOPLE

From the earliest days of the Republic, a person's social class affected his ability to participate in the government and decide its laws. Rome's upper classes, the social elite, were known as patricians. They were born to noble families and were often rich. All other citizens were known as plebeians.

Since the Republic's elected officials were not paid at first, a small group of wealthy patricians held these positions, and as a result, managed to dominate the government. The plebeians struggled against the patricians for more power, and in the 440s B.C., they won an important victory.[1] They forced the patricians to publish the laws of Rome in a document that became known as the Twelve Tables. Now every Roman citizen could learn what the laws—and the punishments for breaking them—were.

Two groups of people were excluded from political affairs: all women, both patrician and plebeian, and slaves. Women were expected to remain home and care for their families, while slaves were considered the property of their masters. As the Roman Empire grew, so did the number of captured enemy soldiers and rebellious residents of the provinces, who were enslaved and brought to Rome.[2]

▶ The Assembly and Senate

During the Republic, Romans were involved in two important government bodies: the Assembly and the Senate. Every male citizen could attend one of four popular assemblies in Rome. At a meeting, which was held outdoors, he could vote

on new laws and elect magistrates. Until 139 B.C., voting was done orally, and then secret ballots were used.

The Senate became very powerful during the Republic. Senators wrote new laws and took them to the assemblies for a vote. They also decided on policies for dealing with foreign nations, and at home they supervised financial matters. As the Republic grew in size, the Senate appointed governors to the newly added provinces and supervised their work. Senators were not elected directly by Rome's citizens. They were men who had previously served as magistrates, the Republic's government officials. All ex-magistrates automatically became senators for life. During the middle years of the Republic (from 264 B.C. to 134 B.C.), there were about three hundred senators.

▷ Consuls and Other Magistrates

There were many types of magistrates in the Republic. Some did legal work, others worked with the Senate on legislation, and still others concerned themselves with religious issues. There were at least two magistrates for each job because the Romans did not want power to be concentrated in the hands of one individual. All magistrates were elected by the assemblies, including the most powerful magistrates— the consuls.

When Rome became a republic in 509 B.C., two consuls, elected for one-year terms, replaced the king. They led the meetings of the Senate, and, more important, each one took charge of an army. In an emergency, the consuls stepped aside to make way for a dictator, who could occupy that position for six months at most. One of the most famous dictators of the Republic was Lucius Quinctius Cincinnatus. According to legend, this hero left his farm to rescue his fellow citizens from a hostile Italian tribe in

The buildings, squares, and temples in Rome known as the Forum were begun during the Republic and greatly expanded during the empire.

458 B.C. He defeated the enemy and sixteen days later returned to his plow.

The government of the Roman Republic was a model of power sharing between the assemblies, the Senate, and the consuls. Each element was supposed to prevent the other two from gaining too much power.

The Government During the Empire

The old institutions of government changed under the dictatorship of the emperor. Some, like the assemblies, were not well adapted to the growing empire. By A.D. 14, at the end of Augustus' reign, there were at least 50 million people within the empire's borders, and many citizens lived too far from Rome to vote.[3] Although the assemblies remained in existence until the third century A.D., they no longer represented the voice of the people.

Back   Forward   Stop   Review   Home   Explore   Favorites   History

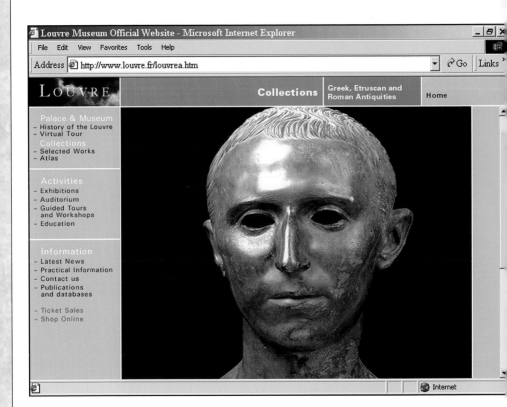

Louvre Museum Official Website - Microsoft Internet Explorer

File   Edit   View   Favorites   Tools   Help

Address http://www.louvre.fr/louvrea.htm   Go   Links

LOUVRE   Collections   Greek, Etruscan and Roman Antiquities   Home

Palace & Museum
- History of the Louvre
- Virtual Tour

Collections
- Selected Works
- Atlas

Activities
- Exhibitions
- Auditorium
- Guided Tours
  and Workshops
- Education

Information
- Latest News
- Practical Information
- Contact us
- Publications
  and databases

- Ticket Sales
- Shop Online

Internet

This bronze bust comes from the Republican period, about 50 B.C.

The Senate gave up a lot of its power to the emperor, but it seemed to grow in size along with the empire. By Constantine's time, there were two Senates, one in Constantinople and one in Rome, each with two thousand members! As for the consuls, they had little power.

Although a citizen had fewer opportunities to participate in the government during the Empire, Romans still valued their citizenship. In fact, the emperor often used citizenship as a reward to gain the loyalty and cooperation of those he conquered. As citizens of the Roman Empire, people in the provinces, such as Greeks, Spaniards, and Syrians, enjoyed the protection of Roman law. Since they were treated as equals, they were less likely to rebel.

THE LANDS AND RELIGIONS OF THE EMPIRE

The Roman Empire grew so much that it eventually touched on all the lands bordering the Mediterranean Sea. The land and its resources varied greatly from one province to the next, as did the people and their religions. Even as the empire was crumbling, however, Christianity was gradually spreading from east to west.

▶ The Western Provinces

Ancient Italy was mostly an agricultural land. It would have been very difficult to farm the mountainous areas of the Alps in the north and the Apennines, a mountain range running down the length of the boot-shaped peninsula. But in the lowlands, Romans grazed cattle on large ranches and grew large crops of grains, such as millet, corn, wheat, and barley as well as peas and beans. Romans made their own wine and olive oil on the peninsula, and a good deal more was imported from Spain.

It took the Romans nearly two hundred years to make Spain a province. By then, Rome's influence could be seen in the network of roads linking Spain's cities and towns to that peninsula and the stone bridges crossing its rivers.[1] Both roads and rivers helped the Romans export Spanish products, including valuable gold, copper, and silver.

The southern regions of Gaul and Germany were dotted with urban centers, such as Marseilles, a port on the Mediterranean Sea. In the more rural areas, grapes and olives were cultivated. North and west of the great

▲ *The Tiber River courses through the city of Rome. It was an important waterway for the ancient Romans because it offered them easy access to the sea.*

plateau called the Massif Central, the heavy soil was devoted to farming, especially grains. There were large cattle ranches in Gaul and also in Britain. Although Britain did not enrich the empire in minerals, it grew enough corn to sometimes feed the Roman troops as far away as those on the Rhine River in Germany.[2]

▷ North Africa and the Eastern Mediterranean

The rich lands of north Africa lay between the Mediterranean Sea to the north, the Sahara Desert to the south, and Egypt to the east. Although the land sometimes needed irrigation when rainfall was low, the region supplied the Romans with an abundance of grain and olive oil. Not everyone farmed in this region, however. Great cities such as Carthage gave the empire lawyers, senators, and writers.

Agriculture flourished in the eastern Mediterranean. Grain was cultivated in coastal areas and in the fertile valley of the Nile River in Egypt. The surplus from Egypt's huge crops was shipped to the city of Rome to feed its people.[3] In Asia Minor, the sheep produced the best wool in the empire, which was exported to Italy.

The Roman Empire now encompassed a region of truly ancient civilizations. Judaea, now modern Israel and Palestine, was the birthplace of Judaism and, much later, of Christianity as well.

The State Religion

The ancient Romans, like the ancient Greeks, believed their world was shaped by many gods, who controlled everything from the rain needed for their crops to victory or defeat in battle. To gain their gods' goodwill, Romans built temples in their honor. Jupiter, their supreme god, was worshiped at a temple on one of the hills overlooking the Forum before the army went on a military expedition. Mars, the father of Romulus, Rome's founder, was at first the god of agriculture but later was worshipped as the god of war. At the Temple of Vesta, the goddess who guarded Roman homes, six young women stood guard over a sacred fire.

Romans called their religion the "state religion" because when Rome was a city-state, the people thought that worshiping these gods would help to keep it safe.

Judaism

Unlike the Romans, the Jews of ancient Judaea believed in one supreme god. Before the rise of Christianity, they were nearly the only people who worshipped one god. During Roman times, their Temple, a large building in the city of Jerusalem, was the most important place of worship.

After the Romans conquered Judaea at the beginning of the first century B.C., they did not interfere with the Jews' worship. Many Jews resented Roman rule, however, and in A.D. 66, they rebelled. Titus ended the revolt in 70, before he became emperor, and destroyed the Temple. That year marked the beginning of the Diaspora, when Jews began leaving Judaea to live in communities scattered throughout the empire.

▷ Christianity

In A.D. 28 or 29, a Jewish carpenter from Nazareth named Jesus began preaching about God in an area north of Jerusalem called Galilee. He claimed to have a relationship with God that was more personal than that experienced by traditional Jews. He preached that God's kingdom would soon be established on Earth. These teachings created both enthusiasm and fear among his listeners.[4]

◁ The remains of the Temple of Vesta, in the Roman Forum. In Roman mythology, Vesta was the goddess of the hearth, or home.

When Jesus traveled south to Jerusalem, some Jewish leaders and Pontius Pilate, the Roman governor of Judaea, arranged to have him arrested and tried for treason. Jesus was nailed to a cross, a punishment that was given to rebels, and died. Soon afterward, his followers spread the word that he was not like other men, because they believed him to be the Son of God.

The earliest believers in Jerusalem thought Jesus' teachings were only for Jews. Paul of Tarsus, a Mediterranean city northwest of Judaea, preached that non-Jews could also become Christians. His view prevailed, and by A.D. 100, there were Christian communities in most important cities of the Roman Empire.[5]

But the Roman Empire under the emperor Nero persecuted early Christians for their beliefs. When a huge and destructive fire burned in Rome in 64, many Romans blamed Nero, a violent man who murdered both his mother and his wife. Nero blamed the fire on the small Christian community in the city of Rome. He rounded up as many Christians as he could and killed them. Christians continued to be persecuted by the Romans under a series of emperors. Finally, in 313, the emperor Constantine announced that Christianity would be legally permitted in the empire.

LIFE IN ANCIENT ROME

Early in the morning of August 24, A.D. 79, the residents of Pompeii, on the west coast of Italy, felt the earth shake. Then they heard a clap of thunder as Mount Vesuvius, a nearby volcano, erupted, shooting hot lava and ash into the sky.[1] Poisonous fumes and thousands of tons of ash settled over the small town.[2] The fumes and ash killed those who did not manage to escape. But all the ash that

http://www.phil.uni-erlangen.de/~p1altar/photo_html/portraet/roemisch/kaiserzeit/privat_1/priv1 - Microso...

File   Edit   View   Favorites   Tools   Help

Address www.phil.uni-erlangen.de/~p1altar/photo_html/portraet/roemisch/kaiserzeit/privat_1/priv18.JPG   ∂ Go   Links

Done   Internet

▲ The statue of an ancient Roman woman of the upper class.

helped to destroy Pompeii also preserved it, leaving an amazingly detailed picture of everyday life in a Roman town. In the ancient ruins are the remains of shops where people worked, houses where they lived, public baths where they went to visit with friends, and theaters where they were entertained. The rhythms of life in Pompeii, which ended so suddenly, were repeated in countless Roman towns and cities.

▷ Family Life

In ancient Rome, marriage partners were usually chosen for young men and women by older relatives. If they were both marrying for the first time, they were likely to be teenagers. A bride might be only thirteen years old.

Weddings were celebrated at the bride's house. After the banquet, the groom would pretend to take the bride out of her mother's arms. Then, in a rowdy procession, the wedding celebrants joked with the couple and escorted them to the groom's house, the bride's new home.[3]

Romans usually lived only with their children rather than in an extended family. Parents tended to be strict because they believed that it helped young people grow strong enough to handle the problems of adult life. In an essay on raising children, Seneca the Younger, a Roman philosopher, wrote, "We must be careful not to let them have fits of anger, but," he added, "we must also be careful not to stifle their individual personalities."[4]

Most parents thought play should be a part of growing up. Babies had rattles, and older children played with marbles and dolls. All sorts of games were played with nuts and boards. Of course, parents were more concerned about their children's education than about their toys.

Education

During the early years of the Republic, fathers taught their sons how to read, write, and use weapons. By about the third century B.C., wealthy and middle-class families sent children between the ages of seven and eleven to an elementary school to learn reading, writing, and arithmetic. School was often held outside under the awning of a shop. A cloth screen might shut out the distractions in the street, but not the noise.[5]

A girl's education ended at age eleven, but boys went on to study Latin and Greek literature. A few boys from wealthy families prepared for a career in politics or law by studying with a *rhetor,* who taught the art of public speaking. At the age of sixteen, the son of a patrician family often became a senator's apprentice for a year.

Food and Drink

A Roman family's diet depended on their social status. Those without much money ate a lot of wheat, which was probably boiled because the poor usually did not have ovens for baking. They also ate beans and leeks, but meat was a luxury. In modest homes, cheap wine and vinegar were common beverages, and both were mixed with water. Romans of all classes disapproved of drinking wine without water. Romans used milk to make cheese, but they did not drink it. They thought only uncivilized people drank milk!

The wealthy drank wine and ate a variety of meats, vegetables, and fish. An invitation from the poet Martial to a friend offers a glimpse of a middle-class Roman's taste and hospitality: "If you are worried about a lonely dinner at home, Toranius, you can come share your hunger with me. If you are accustomed to an appetizer, you won't be

An artist's view of what a street scene in ancient Rome might have looked like includes men and merchants wearing togas, the traditional clothing of the time.

disappointed; there will be cheap Cappadocian lettuce and strong leeks and tuna fish garnished with sliced eggs. . . . We will also have a small sausage served on a bed of white grits [a boiled wheat dish] and pale beans and red bacon."[6]

▷ Clothing and Shelter

Men and women wore togas in early Rome, but eventually togas were worn only by male Roman citizens. The toga was a heavy, expensive garment made from a large piece of white woolen fabric about eighteen feet long. The fabric was draped over the body in a complicated way that was difficult for a man to arrange by himself. Cincinnatus, the great Roman who according to legend became a dictator for sixteen days, always had his wife, Racilia, help him put on his toga. Eventually, a man wore his toga over a tunic, a straight, short-sleeved garment tied at the waist.

When women stopped wearing togas, they wore tunics covered by *stola,* long full dresses with a colored border around the neckline. Children and slaves wore tunics, too.

Romans who lived in towns often lived in stone houses built for single families. The most common style was an atrium house built around a central open area, which at

Wealthy Romans enjoyed activities that ranged from the arts to athletics. This statue depicts the strength and determination of a Roman wrestler.

times had no roof. In cities with the largest populations, such as Rome, many people owned or rented apartments in a private house, above a shop, or in a large apartment building.

Most of the agricultural land in Italy was divided into large tracts that were owned by the wealthy. On these estates the landowner and his family often lived in a large building complex, called a villa, which had enough living space for farmworkers and even for the livestock. Families with small farms and modest incomes lived in simple huts.

Roman Recreation

Romans enjoyed a variety of entertainment, from literary plays to violent combat. The combat, which Romans called "games," took place in large, open-air amphitheaters, which looked like today's football stadiums. Deadly sword fights between gladiators, specially trained men who wore helmets and shields, were very popular. Some gladiators became celebrities, like the one who inspired someone to scrawl on a wall in Pompeii, "Celadus, the

Thracian, makes all the girls sigh."[7] People also liked to watch fights between a variety of wild animals. On the opening day of the enormous Colosseum, an amphitheater in the city of Rome that held about forty-five thousand spectators, five thousand animals waited their turn in cages.

The most popular form of entertainment in ancient Rome was the chariot race. Men raced teams of chariots, each one pulled by four horses, around a U-shaped arena. The races took place in a building called a circus, which had tiers of seats rising away from the arena. In the Circus Maximus in Rome, up to 250,000 people could cheer for their favorite team—the red, blue, white, or green.

The ancient Romans also liked to attend plays. In Pompeii, theatergoers could watch a comedy in a large, open-air building. Poetry lovers could go to the Odeon, a small theater with a roof, to hear a poet read his latest verses.

Public baths offered yet another place for Romans to enjoy themselves. People of all social classes went daily to exercise, soak in the warm water, and socialize with friends. The philosopher Seneca the Younger, who lived above a bathhouse, found the noise distracting. "When the more muscular types are exercising and swinging about lead weights in their hands, and when they are straining themselves . . . I hear groans," he complained.[8]

Chapter 6 ▶

THE LEGACY OF THE ANCIENT ROMANS

The ancient Romans have influenced modern life around the world in countless ways, from the governments that serve the people to the languages they speak, the calendars they keep, and the buildings they construct.

▶ A Government of Checks and Balances

The United States government, with its executive branch headed by the president, and its legislature consisting of two bodies, the Senate and the House of Representatives, is based in part on the organization of the ancient Roman Republic. The United States Senate was directly inspired by the Senate of ancient Rome. Most modern democracies are organized in the same way, so that one branch of government does not become too powerful.

▶ Language and Literature

The ancient Romans spoke Latin. As their empire expanded, that language replaced local languages in many of the provinces. Five languages evolved directly from Latin: French, Spanish, Italian, Portuguese, and Romanian. As a group they are called the Romance languages because their parent language was the language spoken by the Romans. Although English grew out of a different family of languages, many English words, including *art, beauty, justice, space,* and *time* have Latin origins.

Ancient Rome's greatest works of literature are still read today in the original Latin and in translation. Many were written around the time of Augustus' peaceful reign, including the works of Virgil (70–19 B.C.), who is viewed today as ancient Rome's greatest poet.[1] His long epic poem the *Aeneid,* which celebrates the achievements of the empire, is a literary classic. Ovid (43 B.C.–A.D. 17) is known today for his often irreverent poems, which display what modern readers might call "attitude." That explains why Augustus banished Ovid to the eastern Mediterranean region.

Another writer who suffered banishment and then execution was Cicero (106–43 B.C.), considered by many to have been Rome's greatest public speaker and essayist. He

▲ The Pantheon is a prime example of classical Roman architecture. The inscription on the façade refers to M. Agrippa, the Pantheon's builder, who was a friend and colleague of Augustus.

was devoted to preserving the Republic and was not afraid to speak out against anyone he considered a threat. Among his famous speeches were the fourteen he delivered against Marc Antony, which Cicero paid for with his life. Eight hundred of Cicero's letters survive today. They are a valuable source of information on ancient Rome for historians.

The Julian Calendar

Although Julius Caesar is best known for his military genius, his most lasting contribution to modern times was a complicated assortment of changes that he made to the Roman calendar in 46 B.C. The Julian calendar was made up of cycles of three 365-day years, followed by one year of 366 days, or leap year. It is the calendar still in use today. The reason for Caesar's changes was that the calendar had lost its connection with the seasons, and Caesar's alterations meant that summer would always fall in June and winter in December.

Architecture and Engineering

Some of Rome's greatest works in architecture and engineering are still standing and have inspired generations of engineers, builders, and designers. The Pont du Gard still spans the Gard River in graceful arches outside of the French city of Nîmes. It is a beautiful example of the ingenious aqueducts built by the Romans to bring fresh water from miles away into the cities for drinking and bathing.

In the city of Rome, the Pantheon, a temple to all Roman gods, looks very much as it did two thousand years ago, when Hadrian rebuilt it. This masterpiece is crowned by a dome measuring 142 feet across—the widest dome in the world until the twentieth century.[2] The influence of Rome's classical architecture is reflected in many American

▲ *Roman ruins at Leptis Magna, in Libya. Leptis Magna was influenced by Rome for more than six hundred years, beginning with Rome's defeat of Carthage in 202 B.C. The emperor Trajan made Leptis Magna a Roman colony in the second century A.D.*

buildings, including the United States Capitol building in Washington, D.C., and Monticello, the home Thomas Jefferson designed for himself in Virginia.

The ancient Romans have left traces of their civilization and empire all over Europe and beyond. Visitors to northern England can see the remnants of Hadrian's Wall in the countryside. In southern France the ruins of a Roman amphitheater sit just a few miles from a quaint village. In Libya, tourists can walk through entire neighborhoods of the ancient Roman city of Leptis Magna.

▲ The ancient Romans' legacy extends far and wide. Here, the remains of a Roman amphitheater have been preserved in Caerleon, Wales, which was known as the city of the legions when it was the Roman fortress of Isca.

Most modern people do not celebrate war as the Romans did—thank goodness! But they share other elements of ancient Roman culture. Health and fitness, literature, humor, good food, and great architecture are very much appreciated today, just as they were during Hadrian's time. Modern people are also concerned about the rights of citizens. We owe the ancient Romans, and the Greeks before them, a great debt of gratitude for passing down to us their concept of citizenship.

Chapter 1. Caesar's Decision

1. Charles Freeman, *The World of the Romans* (New York: Oxford University Press, 1993), p. 19.

2. Chris Scarre, *The Penguin Historical Atlas of Ancient Rome* (London: Penguin Books, 1995), p. 30.

3. Quoted in Michael Grant, *The Twelve Caesars* (New York: Charles Scribner, 1975), p. 32.

Chapter 2. From Republic to Empire

1. Charles Freeman, *The World of the Romans* (New York: Oxford University Press, 1993), p. 20.

2. Michael Grant, *The Twelve Caesars* (New York: Charles Scribner, 1975), p. 33.

3. Quoted in Moses Hadas, ed., *A History of Rome from Its Origins to 529 A.D. As Told by the Roman Historians* (New York: Doubleday, 1956), p. 80.

4. Grant, p. 50.

5. Freeman, p. 6.

6. Chester G. Starr, *The Ancient Romans* (New York: Oxford University Press, 1971), p. 27.

7. Freeman, p. 65.

8. Ibid., p. 174.

Chapter 3. The Republican Government and Its People

1. Charles Freeman, *The World of the Romans* (New York: Oxford University Press, 1993), p. 7.

2. Jo-Ann Shelton, *As the Romans Did: A Sourcebook in Roman Social History* (New York: Oxford University Press, 1988), p. 168.

3. Lesley Adkins and Roy A. Adkins, *Handbook to Life in Ancient Rome* (New York: Oxford University Press, 1998), p. 341.

Chapter 4. The Lands and Religions of the Empire

1. Chris Scarre, *The Penguin Historical Atlas of Ancient Rome* (London: Penguin Books, 1995), p. 84.

2. Tim Cornell and John Matthews, *Atlas of the Roman World* (New York: Facts on File, 1982), p. 134.

3. Scarre, p. 74.

4. Charles Freeman, *The World of the Romans* (New York: Oxford University Press, 1993), p. 85.

5. Chester G. Starr, *The Ancient Romans* (New York: Oxford University Press, 1971), p. 187.

Chapter 5. Life in Ancient Rome

1. Robert Etienne, *Pompeii: The Day a City Died,* trans. Caroline Palmer (New York: Harry Abrams, 1992), inside cover.

2. Charles Freeman, *The World of the Romans* (New York: Oxford University Press, 1993), p. 132.

3. Florence Dupont, *Daily Life in Ancient Rome,* trans. Christopher Woodall (Oxford: Blackwell, 1992), p. 109.

4. Quoted in Jo-Ann Shelton, *As the Romans Did: A Sourcebook in Roman Social History* (New York: Oxford University Press, 1988), p. 31.

5. Jérôme Carcopino, *Daily Life in Ancient Rome: The People and the City at the Height of the Empire,* ed. Henry T. Rowell, trans. E. O. Lorimer (New Haven, Conn.: Yale University Press, 1968), p. 105.

6. Quoted in Jo-Ann Shelton, p. 83.

7. Freeman, p. 73.

8. Shelton, p. 314.

Chapter 6. The Legacy of the Ancient Romans

1. Charles Freeman, *The World of the Romans* (New York: Oxford University Press, 1993), p. 187.

2. Ibid., p. 88.

Further Reading

Barter, James. *Julius Caesar and Ancient Rome in World History.* Berkeley Heights, N.J.: Enslow Publishers, Inc., 2001.

Biesty, Stephen. *Rome: In Spectacular Cross Section.* San Diego: Lucent Books, 2001.

Conti, Flavio. *A Profile of Ancient Rome.* Los Angeles: J. Paul Getty Museum, 2003.

Corbishley, Mike. *Ancient Rome.* New York: Facts on File, 2003.

Harris, Jacqueline L. *Science in Ancient Rome.* New York: Franklin Watts, 1998.

Hinds, Kathryn. *The Ancient Romans.* Tarrytown, N.Y.: Benchmark Books, 1997.

Mellor, Ronald, and Marni McGee. *The Ancient Roman World.* New York: Oxford University Press, 2004.

Nardo, Don. *A Travel Guide to Ancient Rome.* San Diego: Lucent Books, 2003.

——. *Women of Ancient Rome.* San Diego: Lucent Books, 2003.

Tames, Richard. *Ancient Roman Children.* Chicago: Heinemann Library, 2003.

Thorne, James. *Julius Caesar: Conqueror and Dictator.* New York: Rosen Publishing Group, 2003.

Index